2/9/59

D0640693

Iona
Henry

IONA HENRY is the daughter of a Methodist minister and she married the son of a Methodist minister. She is a graduate of Baker University in Kansas, has the Master of Arts degree from New York University, and is a graduate fellow in general education at the University of Kansas City where she is working toward a doctorate in English. She has taught at Pfeiffer College in North Carolina and Fairleigh Dickinson University in New Jersey.

FRANK S. MEAD is widely known by the church people of America. He has been a pastor, ordained in the Methodist Church and serving churches in New York and New Jersey, and guest preacher in outstanding American pulpits. Former editor of *Christian Herald,* he has written seven books, including *Handbook of the Denominations,* and is editor of the popular annual, *Tarbell's Teachers' Guide.*

TRIUMPH

OVER

TRAGEDY

TRIUMPH

OVER

TRAGEDY

Iona Henry

with

Frank S. Mead

FLEMING H. REVELL COMPANY

Westwood, N. J.—316 Third Avenue
London E. C. 4—29 Ludgate Hill
Glasgow C. 2—229 Bothwell Street

To

Dad Henry,

who came to meet me

in the valley

with God's lantern

in his hand

CONTENTS

Acknowledgment:

We are especially grateful for the cooperation of St. Elizabeth's Hospital in Granite City, Illinois, in making available to us the complete hospital record of Iona Henry, which begins with the words, "This 42-year-old female is admitted to the hospital after the auto in which she was riding collided with a train near Peters Station. Patient was admitted via the emergency room, and on admission her blood pressure was 0/0. . . ."

The Authors.

TRIUMPH

OVER

TRAGEDY

I

Journey's End

It began when we lost Jane.

Jane died in a New Jersey hospital. Pete and I, the stunned and silent parents, sat in a sun parlor near her room, but there was no sun. Outside, a mid-March storm slashed the rain against the windows; inside, a storm fierce and strange raged in my heart. We watched, as from

13

another world, the grim efficient hurrying of nurses and doctors as they fought their running battle with death.

A doctor would come periodically and say, "The news is . . . bad." He'd go out and I'd go back to my private war with God. Jane, I told God, was only fourteen—too young for anyone to die with a tumor on the brain. I begged for mercy from God and I argued; I even threatened Him—anything to save Jane!

Suddenly it was all over. Beloved Bill Rodda, our pastor, told us simply, "She's gone." We put on our coats and moved like wooden automatons out to our cars in the parking lot, under the cold blinking stars. It was 3 A.M.

We drove the ten miles to our home in Chatham without a word. Bill Rodda drove ahead of us. When we came to the crossing where he must turn off for his home next to the little church on Centre Street, he stopped, came back and grasped our hands. Not a word was spoken, but no prayer was ever more eloquent. Then Pete and I went on alone.

As we pulled into the driveway, we found a note from a women's group of the church

14

pinned on the garage door; they wanted us to know that they were praying for Jane. I just stared at it. I wondered if God had seen it.

We had sent Jack, our ten-year-old son, to spend the night with a neighbor; at ten, he was hardly old enough to face the ordeal of the hospital. He had breakfast over there, and when he came home we told him. He wouldn't believe us. "You're kiddin'," he said.

When he realized that we were serious, he turned and ran into the library and began kicking the furniture. Like mother, like son: Jack was fighting God.

Up to now, our family had been able to handle anything that came to us. We had hurdled many an obstacle, and found a family spirit and unity that conquered whatever had to be conquered. But now—now here was a hard, bitter thing that had driven us to stand with our backs to the wall. I thought in those hours of a friend, a Latvian D.P., who had suffered terribly; when I asked him why he and his family had done nothing in their times of travail, he replied, "Sometimes there is *nossing* to do!" I knew what he meant now, and so did Jack. All he could do,

15

in his futile rage, was to kick the furniture; all I could do was to lash out at God.

After his battle came the release of tears, and then the plans. We told him of the things that must be done—the casket to choose, the cemetery plot to be selected. Would he rather go to his friend's house while we took care of it?

"Nope," said Jack. "I want to be with you."

He went with us, and I am glad he did. It is best to let the child walk through this experience with you. I'm sure he feels more secure in such an experience, searching for maturity with his parents, than he would if they were to shut him out of their plans in a vain desire to shield him from reality.

Jack grew tremendously, in those hours. He picked the cemetery lot—one with a pink dogwood at its foot. "That'll be pretty in the spring," he said. "And if any guy dares walk on it, I'll knock his block off."

The funeral was an affirmation of faith. Our two minister friends, Bill Rodda and Dr. Ev Hallock, were mercifully brief, and the host of friends were thoughtful and kind. They beat a path to the house, when it was all over.

All this was in March of 1952. Easter was just ahead. Easter! How would we ever get through *that*, through the day that had always meant singing and joy? What did we have to sing about now?

We were numb, walking through the days in a trance. Pete, who had always been the staunch heart of the family—the husky, kindly "boss" who could always resolve any problem with his "O.K. Let's go!"—Pete went to his work like a galley slave. The men at the Swift plant in Harrison, where he was division superintendent, helped him all they could and sent him home early and talked of his taking a vacation. His heart was so heavy with the chains of grief that his whole being was drugged and inert.

It was like that for me, too, in the house. The house was filled with a dark, spiritless emptiness, interrupted only by the sight of something that brought an ache deeper than tears. In every room I saw something that reminded me. . . .

That's the desolating thing about death. The passing is hard enough, but it is the emptiness that is left behind that crushes us.

Out of the emptiness came an idea: why not

17

go out to Wichita and visit Dad and Mother Henry? Dad Henry (Pete's father) was a minister —one of those rare ministers who can walk into a room and make you feel better, without saying a word. We'd go there. It would get us away from the house, away from the bitterness and the constant reminding. It would be good to sit and talk with Dad Henry. If anyone on earth could help us, he could.

We discussed it with Dr. Dochtermann, our Chatham physician, and finally decided to drive. Driving would be better than sitting in a train or plane and thinking. It would be better if we drove; then we would have something to do.

We left Chatham early on the morning of April fifth and drove until dark, so that we would be tired enough to sleep. The sixth was more of the same: silent, dreary, seemingly endless driving. We slept the night of the sixth in a little motel—I haven't the least idea where it was—and started out early on the morning of the seventh. We had a hasty breakfast just a few miles out of East St. Louis. We had no reason to be hasty about it; we were just glad to get it over with, and get out on the road.

18

This was the last day of the trip—journey's end! By nightfall we would be with the family. Jack was in the back seat, lonesome without Jane, who always rode with him; Pete drove, and I sat beside him with the road maps in my lap. We were all thinking of Jane, all vaguely conscious of the country around us but not particularly interested in it. We approached a railroad crossing.

Down the track, a hundred feet away, Train 47, a fast freight of the Nickel Plate Railroad, also approached the crossing. We never saw it.

The rest is a blank; I remember nothing, and I'm grateful to God for that. I was told that the train struck us at a speed of fifty miles an hour; it took the engineer nearly half a mile to stop.

Pete and Jack were killed instantly and I was hurled forty feet down the right-of-way.

If we had spent two minutes longer at breakfast, it would never have happened!

The ambulance men came and rolled me on a stretcher. They must have wondered whether it was worthwhile taking me to the hospital at all. I was already dead, or so near dead that no human hand could measure the distance. . . .

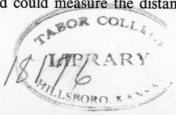

II

The Valley of the Shadow

For the next few days, we'll have to look at the hospital record.

The doctor and the nurses in the emergency room at St. Elizabeth's Hospital, in Granite City, Illinois, couldn't tell at first whether I was white or Negro, I was so covered with oil, grime, cinders and blood. They sent for a priest, and began to write down the record of what was broken in me.

Dr. Bowers wrote down something like this:

Concussion—six-inch laceration right side of forehead.

Fracture of right clavicle.

Fracture of all ribs.

Puncture of the right lung.

Double fracture of right humerus.

Tearing of ligaments of right knee. Lower right leg is turned outward almost at a right angle.

Fracture of right ankle.

Multiple pelvis fractures.

Multiple deep lacerations.

Dirt ground into the tissues and into the periosteum of the bone.

He felt for my pulse, and could get no pulse. He listened with his stethoscope and could get only a faint heart beat. He tried to get my blood pressure, and wrote on his chart "Zero over zero." No blood pressure. But there was a temperature. That was about all there was.

A priest came. I did not see him in that room, nor do I remember anything he said or did. He gave me the last rites of his faith, and they told me later that I rallied for a moment after that was done and asked if we might repeat the Lord's Prayer together. He nodded, and bent low over my lips as we went through it. The priest finished the Prayer with the words ". . . but deliver us from evil." I went on to whisper, "For thine is the kingdom and the power and the glory. . . ."

Then it was that they knew I was Protestant. It meant nothing to them, nor to anyone else as long as I was in that hospital. I was a dying stranger and they took me in and did for me what they knew God would expect them to do.

I was given glucose and two pints of blood, and put to bed.

Insofar as those about me were concerned, I was in bed. Insofar as I was concerned, I was on the thin boundary line that separates this world from the next, and I knew it. Pete and Jack were there. They said things—not with their lips but with their eyes. It was all with the eyes, yet it was as real and clear as any words I have ever heard from human lips. They would come close and recede and then come back again. There was a longing and a loving and an urging me to come with them, in their eyes. It was no dream; it was reality. I kept asking myself, "Why isn't Jane with them? Where is *she*?"

I used to smile at people who told me stories like this—stories of being almost dead but not quite, of wandering back and forth across the line that separates life and death, and of seeing their lost loved ones over there beyond the line. I laugh no longer. It has happened to me.

The hospital record reads: "Patient is semi-conscious; she talks coherently at times but then seems to lapse into a coma." What is "conscious," and "unconscious" and "semiconscious"? Where is the man, the doctor or scientist or metaphysician, who can tell where one begins and the others end? Conscious? I was supposed to be conscious as I lay at the side of the Nickel-Plate tracks and carried on a conversation with a police officer, giving him our names and addresses and destination; not until the ambulance men lifted me did the policeman realize that I was really *unconscious*, for I did not cry out in pain when they moved my broken bones.

How do you explain it? Did my unconscious mind do what my conscious mind had set up a pattern of doing over the years, or was I, in conscious moments, guided by an unconscious force? Whatever the answer, I know this: *there is a greater Power within us than we ever realize or understand, and the line between the worlds of visible and invisible, conscious and unconscious, is the thinnest of all lines and is crossed quickly and easily.*

I also know this: there is nothing difficult or complicated about dying. It is easy, simple, painless release. I believe with Whittier, since this experience of mine, that death is no more than

> *. . . a covered way*
> *Which opens to the light*
> *Wherein no blinded child can stray*
> *Beyond the Father's sight.*

They slipped me into a hospital bed and told each other that it wouldn't be long. I'd die there, very soon.

They started looking around for a special nurse but it was difficult to find one. Naturally! Who wanted a job like this? Why fight for the life of one already half dead?

Chatham was stunned, when the news came back. People couldn't believe it. First Jane, then

Pete and Jack, and tomorrow—me. It was one of those things that just couldn't happen in such happy towns and among such happy people.

This was Holy Week, and Bill Rodda had more than enough to do; this is the busiest season of any preacher's year. But the ecclesiastical routine, for once, was completely overshadowed and destroyed by something that had happened in Granite City, Illinois!

Bill's phone rang incessantly; people stopped him on the street to ask him how I was. Out of nowhere, automatically, a "fund" was started —money began to trickle in to buy Bill Rodda a plane ticket to Granite City, Illinois.

Bill caught a plane. It is nearly 1500 miles from Chatham, New Jersey, to Granite City, as the crow flies and God guides the planes.

Others came flying from other directions; how quickly do human love and sympathy find wings! On Wednesday morning, while I was still "out," my brothers, Chuck and Franklin, arrived. Bill Rodda came to the hospital with them, but he stood in the corridor outside the room when they came in to stand at the side of the bed. They say I greeted each brother with "Hello, Franklin. . . . Hello, Chuck . . ." and then, cocking my head toward the corridor back of my bed, I said "Hello, Bill!" Startled, they all realized that no one had told me that Bill Rodda was in Granite City, much less out there in the corridor. How did I know Bill was there? Only God can answer that one.

Dad and Mother Henry came, to stand in stricken silence looking down at only one of the three they had been waiting to welcome in Wichita. Dad left me only once—to go back to Chatham, with the bodies of his son and grandson.

Twenty-four hours later, things cleared for just a moment and the reality of the other world that had engulfed me gave way to another reality. I awoke, and for the first time saw clearly the face of my minister, who had come more than a thousand miles to stand at the side of that bed. He had been there for two days, and I had not seen him, but I knew. . . .

I said to him, "Pete's gone." It wasn't a question; it was a statement of fact. Bill hesitated a moment, and then he nodded.

"And Jack's gone, too." He nodded again. As I tried to twist my pain-tortured head away from him, he said slowly, "Listen to me. I am here because Pete and Jack couldn't be here; your friends in Chatham insisted that I come. They are saying through me, 'Iona, you've *got* to get well, and come back.' I was sent to tell you that you *must* get well. They are counting on you—and you can't let them down."

I grasped it, vaguely, and it was good to grasp. Then the soft black waves rolled over me and I went down again, and knew no more.

Imagine a broken, inert body rising and sinking in the sea. Now it comes slowly to the surface; now it is sunk again into the dark, cool depths. This was exactly my reaction, for four long days. I wanted to go down and stay down —I wanted to die. I asked God to let me die. Why not? Why suffer with this unbelievably broken body, to no purpose at all? Why live? All I had to live for had been wiped out. The years ahead could hold only emptiness past bearing.

27

Take me, God! If I had any thought at all in my conscious moments, it was this. I was too numb and weary and sick to think anything else.

But above me hovered the face of Bill Rodda, sent by my friends a thousand miles away; above me were the faces of doctor and nurse who were resolved that I should *not* die.

III

The Battle with Pain

Now came pain.

It wasn't so bad when I slept—either from exhaustion or under sedative—for then Pete and Jack came to me, and the hurting disappeared. But I would wake out of that to the sensation of a wall tumbling in on me—to searing, grinding, grating pain. It was so fierce that I could only lie there gasping, as I stared up at the ceiling. Never in my life had I known such agony.

Dad and Mother Henry, who were at my side during these days, suffered heartbreak as they watched fingers claw at the bandages and pull at the slings and casts, fighting to get free, moaning, struggling, collapsing.

No prisoner was ever so bound and shackled as I was in that bed. My right arm was suspended in traction; a long cast sheathed my right leg, from hip to ankle; rib belts were wound tightly around my body, and I was swung clear of the bed in a pelvic sling that reached from shoulder to hips. My head was swathed in bandages above the eyes; below the eyes, every now and then, they strapped on an oxygen mask. And the only free parts of me—the left arm and leg—became the channels through which all transfusions, life-giving glucose and blood, were poured into me.

There I dangled, helpless, between bed and ceiling, unable to move. I was also dangling helpless between two worlds, terrifyingly unable to think clearly about either of them. In those hours I developed an everlasting sympathy with those who wander in the shifting shadows of mental illness. I even prayed that my brain would collapse under the strain, so that I would not have to face the reality of the new life which awaited me if I got well.

I would feel myself completely removed from the familiar, and go roaming dismally in a land of pure fantasy; then I would wake and look around me at the room and the people in it and long to get back into the dream world, for it was far more desirable than the waking world so filled with pain.

My constant desire in those dream hours was to get home to care for my husband and children. I would actually be on the way home—only to open my eyes and find myself still in the bed, still in this world, and still haunted by the awful knowledge that I couldn't go home because there wasn't any home, any husband or children. No plans were possible because the reasons for planning had vanished. The patterns of twenty years of domestic living suddenly were broken and, I realize now, as these patterns broke, my mind was threatened with breaking, too.

So there I was, suspended between life and death. I was like Nolan, in *The Man Without a*

Country, sentenced to sail forever in a ship without port, without hope, without roots or homeland anywhere. I fought to die. At least, in dying, I would go in *one* direction, and not just dangle there.

The faces of Chuck and Bill Rodda went in and out of the mists and then I began to see another face, a strange face but a constant face. He spoke strange words to me that yet had a familiar tone to them, like a bell heard ringing far off in the distance. It was Dr. Bowers. He said, "I know you don't want to get well, but I'm working hard to heal you, for I'm convinced you were saved for some purpose. I want you to help me work out that purpose."

Slowly, each word deliberately, carefully chosen, his message burned into my brain. Purpose! How grotesque. How almost enormously *funny*! And yet his patient manner, his kind eyes, his humble sincerity called up from deep within me an answering response and grudgingly, conditionally, I murmured an assent.

I began to understand that there were nurses in the room; the glowing white of their uniforms seemed like candles moving in the murky shad-

32

ows of a cathedral. I learned that one of them had left her home and husband and two children to come and do what she could for a woman about to die. She symbolized a gallant something that is the antithesis of pain. I'm not sure just what it is, but this I know about it: it reaches for the sufferer the minute the suffering begins. God and human sympathy are still the greatest ambulance chasers in America; they reach the hospital together, one coming down the bleak road of pain, the other via the shining path on which love and sympathy have right-of-way, *sans* speed laws and traffic lights.

In the morning came a drill-sergeant of a nurse who took the day's orders from the doctor and saw to it that they were obeyed. With a precision almost military, she got the routine under way, taking the orders and valiantly executing them. Routine! Have you in hospitals ever stopped to thank God for it? It is the most prosaic element in healing. It is unshakable, undeviating. It bows to no one and to nothing—not to mental states or emotional turmoil or whims or your ideas of this or that. Hope or heartbreak take second place to the fever thermometer; the stethoscope and the pills arrive at their appointed times though empires totter and fall. There is a time for this and a time for that, and you get into the habit of forgetting your pain a little when it comes time for this or that. Routine is as inevitable, inexorable, in the sickroom and the hospital as dawn and twilight, and I know now that this routine was a strong factor in saving my life, for it diverted my mind from its distress.

This, too, I know: had I lost Pete and Jack and been left physically whole—had I not been in the desperate condition that called for the desperate routine—I am quite sure I could not have stood the shock of their passing. Perhaps routine is one of God's supports against shock.

In the afternoons came a red-haired, rollicking nurse who could have coaxed laughter out of the Man in the Iron Mask. And medically, too, she knew the score. She had nursed wounded and dying soldiers at a base hospital during the Second World War, and when I complained (as I often did) she would come up with a story of some soldier who had suffered much more than I.

34

THE BATTLE WITH PAIN

She taught me a good lesson: when you're sick, a sense of humor will help you as much as pills and thermometers—and maybe more. Strange, isn't it, that nurses, living as they do in constant company with pain, invariably have such a good sense of humor? Perhaps it isn't strange, but inevitable and necessary; perhaps it is all that saves them from going to pieces under strain.

Other nurses had other contributions to make. One was the most cheerful widow I've ever met. I remember watching her one day and thinking, "If I could be as cheerful a widow as she is, maybe. . . ." She seemed so normal and content. Another had an Irish brogue so thick you could cut it with a dull knife. Her salty retort to my complaining was "Sure, and is it more miracles you're wanting? Haven't ye had enough, without askin' the good Lord for more?"

It was a good day when the Creator made nurses.

After the fourth day, the pain-shot hours began to mean "time"—something that had stopped while I was in coma. I was conscious now of daylight and dark, of one day following another. The rising-and-sinking-in-the-sea sensation left me; in its place came the sensation of walking through dark valleys. They stretched far ahead, and always just beyond them were gloomy, formidable mountain peaks. Always, those mountains lay there, waiting for me to climb them.

I asked for a calendar. A calendar, up on the wall where I could see it and count the days. Everyone agreed with me that it would be nice to have a calendar—but somehow it was always forgotten. Of course it was forgotten! A calendar would have been the worst possible thing; it would have made time stretch out to unbearable distance.

So the days wore on, and under the onslaught of drugs and constant medical care, the pain began to moderate. The medical record speaks of "Penicillin" and of "Demerol (given for eighty-three days)." And of streptomycin, cremadiazine, and sulfa drugs. Needles, pills. Oxygen, for seven days. A medical merry-go-round, and I was conscious only of a dizzy ride I wished would stop.

36

THE BATTLE WITH PAIN

It nearly did stop, I found out later, on the fifteenth day. A swelling where there had been none before, a new agony of pain in the damaged leg, a skyrocketing fever—all these were new red flags of danger to the doctor and nurses. Off came the leg cast; the family was told that it was either an embolus, which could mean amputation, or a phlebitis, which could possibly cause death. Which was worse?

It was that bad; the nurses whispered, "This is *it*." This could be the end of it. But. . . .

Within twenty-four hours the leg began to heal.

One by one, the shackles were removed. The rib belt came off at the end of twenty days; the immobilized leg lost its tight "ace" bandage on the thirty-sixth day, the pelvic sling went on the fortieth day and the arm came out of traction after sixty days. With the help of drugs, deity and the doctor, we were slowly winning the battle against pain.

When the family tried to express their thanks to Dr. Bowers for his part in it he replied, "Don't thank me. Thank the Man Upstairs. I think God works through the doctor."

The Man Upstairs, to be sure, had much to do with it. He came quickly, and so did His personal representatives.

There were Sisters in the hospital. They moved in and out of my room and my consciousness like benedictions in black, moving quietly, surely, almost happily, standing in silent or softly spoken prayer with the compassion of a suffering Christ upon them like light. Lovely in their midst was Sister Petronella, who must have been in her late seventies; she was "retired"—and giving full time to a ministry of healing in the hospital that had nothing to do with scalpels and drugs. Her tools were faith, hope and love. She pointed my eyes to a crucifix on the wall and said, "I hope that my Friend up there will be your Friend, too." I could only mumble that He and I had been friends for a long, long time, and she left the room, smiling and content.

They moved like gentle wraiths, these Sisters, in and out, day and night. They were a part of the divine compassion; without them, the pain would have been far worse.

The ministers of every church in Granite City came to pray in my room; often, there were laymen or laywomen praying, too. They were Methodists, Presbyterians, Baptists, Pentecostalists, Roman Catholics. Formal or informal, they all opened their hearts and prayed simply and beautifully and very, very humbly, and I was lifted up and strengthened.

The churches of the city prayed for me, at morning and evening service; their members sent me gifts and little cards with Scripture verses typed or scrawled in longhand. Twice, thrice a day the Sisters came to pray briefly. In the mails came prayers and tracts from Christian Scientists, from Unity, from Jews, from conservative Christian and liberal Christian, from the whole wide praying range that ran from a child in a backwoods wilderness church to the pastor of a metropolitan congregation.

The sling in which my body was suspended became a bulletin board on which were pinned these words of cheer and hope from His messengers. A prayer from Ev Hallock, in Rutherford, was typical; I read it often: "Dear God, when I suffer with my Lord and cry out, 'Why?' may I also cry out, 'Father, into thy hands I commend my spirit. . . .' Such trust, such confidence was

39

in Jesus, and it can be mine. Let me have it, Father, and with it Thy help and strength, Thy comfort and peace, until I glorify Thy name in the spirit of the Great Physician. . . ."

All of this, all of these, helped me overcome the pain of the spirit—helped me to lift my eyes to the Friend on the crucifix and marvel how He had brought me through the valley of the shadow of death. I'd fall asleep remembering His words, "Lo, I am with you alway, even unto the end of the world."

There is always, in sickness, a pain born of loneliness. It is especially sharp for one a thousand miles from home, as I was—yet the long arm of love spanned those miles as though they never existed.

A network of communications from Granite City to Harrison, New Jersey, to Chicago had alerted Swift and Company, and almost before I was out of the emergency room the General Superintendent's office had Superintendent Lou Horwich of the East St. Louis plant on the telephone:

"Pete Henry's wife is in the hospital. Go to

her. Go *now*. See that she gets whatever she needs. Never mind the expense. Get it, and fast. And take care of Pete and Jack. . . ."

Lou Horwich dropped everything, and came. He took charge; he took care of large items and small details; nothing escaped him. He and his wife, neither of whom had hardly known I existed, before the crash, came and stayed; they were still helping the day I left the hospital! They never let me be lonely.

Swift's supervised the financial department; out of Pete's account they paid the bills and they even sent a case of dog-food to Stormy, our dog in Chatham, every two weeks! Don't ever tell me that big business is "cold and impersonal."

A few days after the crisis with the right leg, Dr. Dochtermann walked into the room. I had not sent for him. This trip from Chatham was his own idea, and he came at his own expense. We talked. He told me about Chatham, of how things were going in the old world I had left so far behind, how the boys in the Hi-Y were cutting the lawn each week, how the police were watching things for me, night and day. The old ways still existed; the old friends were still there.

41

This doctor sitting in my room was symbol of them all, speaking for them all as, without words, he was asking me to come back.

He left me, once, for a half-hour or so. I did not know until weeks later that he went down to the blood bank to give a pint of his blood. His explanation was interesting: "She has enough flowers. I thought it might be better to put a little blood in the bank, just in case. . . ."

He was right about the flowers. I had enough flowers. They came from all points of the compass, in a fragrant flood—from Chatham, Granite City, points in between and far beyond, from friends, from total strangers trying to tell me that they were with me, in the buds and blooms. Who can ever forget flowers in the hospital? They have a mute, miraculous therapy. The sight of a rose sent by one who is trying to tell you that he loves you can smother the pain of a broken bone.

Then Dr. Dochtermann went home and a lot of my loneliness went with him, never to return.

There were cards, of course, thousands of

them. One of the nurses elected herself "social secretary," and saw to it that I saw and read every card. She also supervised the opening of the presents; that was a ritual every evening at seven. The nurse made a gay excitement of it: "Which one shall we open first?"

Thank God for cards and presents! They are a radiant barrage against sick-room loneliness, and their power is greater than we think. Their power lies not so much in themselves as in the thought that people don't forget!

Only once did a present hurt. The nurse found it one night as she sorted out some things which had been in my luggage—a little pin Jack had given me for a birthday present. I broke into tears. It took the nurse to save that day with the words, "You shouldn't feel that way. Don't you see—it's Jack's Mother's Day present to you." The next day was Mother's Day. I wore the pin, proud and happy.

So Jack reached out of the past to help fight my sense of loneliness. . . .

By mid-May the hospital employees had begun to visit my room—a happy parade of gloomdispellers. One had lost her husband, and was left with four children! She was much, much worse off than I, and my heart forgot its own selfish pain to go out to her. Another had a startlingly realistic philosophy; she said, "It's a good thing the world is round instead of square. If it were square we'd come to the place, sooner or later, where we couldn't go any further. But since it's round, we just keep on going." She knew what she was talking about; she had lost to death almost as much as I.

Mary was Croatian: she spoke only one word of English to ten of Croat, but she could nevertheless spin long, passionate tales of her daily doings. She brought gifts—gifts without end and grapes wrapped in swathes of old newspapers— over which I enthused long and properly. Her final gift, just before I left the hospital, was a lovely slip—size forty-two for my 100-pound frame! To her question, "It fit?" I lied joyfully: "Perfectly!"

What a democracy a hospital is! What a *school* it is! Lesson No. 1, more people bear pain in this world than do not, and there are different ways of bearing it. Lesson No. 2, you

44

are never alone in pain in a hospital or anywhere else; you are a member of a very, very inclusive fraternity. Lesson No. 3, there is fun to be had in life's most unexpected places—even here, within a few feet of the operating room!

Gradually, the pain lessened. But still I kept on taking demerol, for with demerol I was sure of sleep. The doctor began suggesting that I stop it, but I begged for it, just a little while longer. It was the one drug that brought sleep, without fail.

Of course, pain was not so much a problem now, as was the *mind*. I feared my memories and I had no future worth thinking about, so I sought escape in demerol-sleep.

It did no good for the doctor to tell me that I *had* to learn to sleep on my own; I just couldn't sleep on my own. One day the nurse came to me and whispered mysteriously, "I heard something *awful* about you today, in the nurses' dining room." She shook her head at the thought of it; it was just too terrible for words. I was curious, then almost angry, as the mystery persisted. "*Tell* me! What did you hear?"

"The nurses—they're saying that you're becoming a dope addict."

"A *dope* addict?"

"That's it. You're sunk, with that demerol. It becomes habit forming—and you've been on the stuff for eighty-three days. Some of those days, you had several shots."

She looked at me like a sorrowing mother looking at her wayward child starting for reform school. Too bad, too bad!

Never in my life have I been so completely angry as I was at that moment; I was so furious I could hardly speak. I blazed. Dope addict, was I? So *that's* what they're saying behind my back. Well, I'll show 'em. I'll show those smart nurses that there is a will power in me stronger than anything their medical science knows about. I'll show 'em.

What I didn't know was that they were using a reverse psychology on me. They and the doctor had made plans to push me, shove me into a fight with demerol. It worked.

In a beautiful fit of rage I picked up a book I had been reading, and I was deeply engrossed in it by the time night came. It was one of the

46

hottest nights the St. Louis area had ever known, and it seemed to me that all the heat in the world was directed at me. My bed was soaking wet with perspiration and heat-inspired misery was added to my hate-inspired rebellion against the nurses' edict, when two innocent little student nurses came with the demerol. They stood wide-eyed when I refused it. One of them stammered, "The doctor *ordered* it." I raged: "I don't care if he did. Take it away." They looked at each other, and started out of the room, still in possession of the demerol.

Then one of them came back to the bed, patted my hand and said, "Never mind, honey. If you don't sleep tonight, you will tomorrow night." What tact! She should get a Florence Nightingale medal for that: it was *exactly* the thing to say, for it was exactly right.

The night wore on, hotter and hotter. My light stayed on; propped up in bed, I stuck to the book. As I dashed away the perspiration I got to thinking of the three Hebrew boys who had been put in the fiery furnace because they would not bow down to the heathen gods—and I laughed out loud. The nurses undoubtedly thought I had gone out of my mind, in this fight to the finish with demerol, but they were good enough not to say so. They came by and looked at me, and went on. I went back to the three boys in the furnace, and something came from them to me that was not funny. I heard them say, "Our God . . . is able to deliver us from the burning fiery furnace. . . . But if not . . . we will not. . . ." If not, then I'd *die* before I'd call for that shot of demerol. I set my teeth and tossed in the bed, picked up the book and put it down, wanted to give in a dozen times—and then, just before dawn, I dozed off. When I awoke I was greeted like a victorious queen receiving her royal court.

"She's done it!"

The next night, I slept.

Conquering demerol was, I think, the real victory over pain. I was so thrilled at the thought of it that I wanted to get out of bed and run up and down the halls, shouting my joy. This hard thing I had done, on my own. And if I could do that, I could do anything.

The rest of the battle with pain was easier, much easier. It was like a series of short little skirmishes with the rear guard of suffering, after the main engagement had been won. On the seventy-third day one of the nurses looked at me and said, "I think you'll make it, now. No temperature for twenty-four hours. You'll make it now."

"What? Didn't you think I'd make it, all along?"

"We didn't know. A temperature means anything can happen, any time. And you've had temperature. Until today. It's gone now."

Pain? I know pain. You will know it, meet it, fight it, whoever you are. You must. It is a law of life that you just face pain. But this I have learned, in my fight with it: it is given to produce something better than tears and frustration. It produces love, sympathy and a brotherhood that is more spiritual than physical. There is deep purpose in pain; it opens our eyes to the methods of God with men. It brings out of the heart and mind the finest that God has put there. It sets deep calling unto deep, from heart to heart to heart, in direct reply to the call of God.

So we might sing a Te Deum to pain!

IV

The Battle with Fear

Pain is a brute, but you have to admit that it
fights in the open, in the broad light of day.
You can find pain and face it and fight it, for
you know just where it is. But with fear it's
different.

Fear is a sneak, an artist at the sneak attack.
It hovers under the cover of pain; it strikes in

the dark, in low moments when you are least ready to meet it. And you fight it alone, inside. There are no drugs to conquer fear.

Like pain, fear is inevitable. It comes to all of us, in one form or another. Whoever you are, wherever you are, some day you will have to meet it and beat it, unless you want it to beat you.

It can be beaten, if you are smart enough to accept the help of certain allies. Mature people who face their problems can whip fear if they want to.

Fear struck at me out of the darkness before the pain was gone; the agony of broken bones hid, but not for long, the leering, ugly faces of insecurity and alarm about the future. It was not fear of death; the human body can stand just so much pain, and then death takes on the mien of welcome release. I would have liked to die for I had been near enough to it to sense the calm, quiet beauty of death.

It was in the first hours of waning pain that I began to feel the little daggers of fear stabbing into my spirit. Here I was safe and secure in a hospital room, safe at least as long as I was there from the ruthless, merciless world that had shattered my life. Here a corps of doctors and nurses and friends and a high wall of love and sympathy stood between me and the blows of human life.

But there grew in my heart a gnawing, paralyzing knowledge that some day I would have to leave that room and go back. When that thought came, fear was its co-partner.

It is like that with many of us, even when life goes smoothly and painlessly. It is so, especially with a married woman. She spends a great part of her adult life in the companionship of her family. They are close, and every waking hour she thinks of them, and they of her. They have an unsigned treaty against the outside world; the family is the woman's armor against "the slings and arrows of outrageous fortune." Her days and hours are filled with the creature needs of her family. What shall we have for dinner tonight? We'll have to get new shoes for Tommy. What's wrong between daughter and her boy friend? Which college shall we choose for Bill?

But let one—just one—of the family be taken from her, and the protective circle is broken and

52

a weak spot appears in the armor. The break brings the necessity of mending, of setting a totally new pattern of making new and more important decisions on her own.

And here I was, the only one left of a family that had been wiped out! What was I to do *now*? For the first time in my life, I couldn't plan ahead.

The only relief, at first, was in demerol; that brought unconsciousness, and in unconsciousness I couldn't think. Dr. Bowers understood what was happening; he knew that for me to wake and think was almost beyond my strength to endure. He said, compassionately, "Live it just one moment at a time. The past is too raw, the future too far away. One moment at a time— *this* moment."

Drugging yourself into sleep may give you temporary release from pain, but is a shabby weapon against fear. It is too much like the alcoholic drinking himself senseless in order to "get away from himself." The trouble is, the problem is there when he comes back! Fear is a coward, but it hangs around. It persists, waiting until the drug wears off. There is no medicine yet discovered that will outwit fear. You have to get it into the open and face it in fair fight, and beat the life out of it.

In the first days of pain-shot consciousness, before the telegrams and the letters and cards and gifts and love of friends could make itself felt, I learned this: *there are times when we have but one direction in which to turn*. It came to me as I lay there looking up at my hand, suspended on its ropes high in the air. That hand was at first a vague symbol of my reaching for *something*; then it became a visible means of touching the invisible hand of God. My arm fought to stretch higher, higher; my fingers opened and closed and fought to close on something high and lifted up, high above this bed, this pain. I knew I must reach it, *had* to reach it—to survive.

I grasped at last what I strove to reach: the strong right hand of God. I held on fast and looked at the Christ on the wall and whispered, "Yea, though I walk through the valley of the shadow of death, thou art with me. . . ." I understood then that He had brought me through not one valley, but many, and I held fast to the

54

hand hidden from me in the valley. I held, and He did not let me go.

Through my fevered mind began to flow the vibrant assurance of words that once had been only words—lovely, to be sure, but still words whose power I did not know, for up to now I had known no such pain or tragedy. They came to stand between me and my fears like a shining sword: "The eternal God is thy refuge, and underneath are the everlasting arms. . . ." "Leaning, leaning, leaning on the everlasting arms." I leaned, and they did not give way. "But they that wait upon the Lord shall renew their strength; they shall mount up with wings as eagles; they shall run, and not be weary; and *they shall walk, and not faint*." Walk! Walk, walk, walk! *Me?*

It was healing, strengthening power straight from the lips of God. It came like the sight of a sail to an Iona Henry clinging to a life raft in a storm at sea.

This was, I grant, emotional. It came out of a heart as badly broken as my bones, not out of a cool, healthy mind. It was emergency, "foxhole" faith and, I think, was a normal reaction

55

for one in a state of physical shock. But had it continued too long—aye there's the rub—for pure, emotional, "foxhole" faith will not carry you in the long pull. Something much stronger is needed there. But we'll come to that later.

Another fear supplanted the first, more deadly because it was more practical. It was economic. "You'll be a burden to others!" Someone, surely, would have to take care of this cripple for the rest of her life. What right did I have to expect anyone to do that? People had their own lives to live, their own problems to face. I had no right to ask that of anybody—and I could never take care of myself.

The bills made it even worse. Anyone who has had even a slight brush with a hospital knows that bills mount quickly to a size that seems to approximate the national debt. Practical Dad Henry stepped in here and within twenty minutes convinced me, as his son before him would have, that only one thing was necessary: to have me able to leave the hospital as physically strong as possible. "You are going to get well—that's all we care about."

This is the perfect answer to the bill question.

Bills are the steppingstones to health, and they should be recognized as that. Money means nothing, in the end; all that matters is the getting well. We are foolish when we put price tags on that!

I suppose the reason I worried so much about the bills now was that I had never had to worry about them before. Pete had done that. Like most wives, I had been content to let the man of the house carry the financial burden for I had other loads to worry about. I knew very little about money; in that department I was a babe in the woods. I had lived in a woman's world in which the gears that made things run were not dollars but little temporary needs. Pete had lived in a man's world, a world of hardheaded, planning practicality. It was a good thing he had, for he had put away what I needed now. When I realized that, I stopped worrying.

Ed Parker, long-time friend and business-man, came all the way from his home in Mountain Lakes, New Jersey, to stand by my bed and help plan the details of my business world. He did this out of love for my husband, just as many others of Pete's friends aided in other areas.

And what would I have done without them! They were a sort of cushion that protected me from the very abrupt jolt my world received when Pete left it.

Write this down and look at it often: *this is a man's world*, and we women had better accept it as such. Accept it and depend upon its sound advice, for we need it. Especially when our little boat runs onto an economic sand bar, we need it. For out of that man's world come the physical and economic sustenance of life. That department is something men can handle, something they can do, and something they want to do. Let them do it—and go about doing what you can do. A woman's world is filled with other things, other work and interests, other contributions. Each to his own world!

But the fear of "What will I do?" persisted. What would I do, what could I do, when I left the hospital? I had been a mother and a house-wife; now that had been denied me. It would have to be something else. But what? And suddenly there came a letter from Dr. Peter Sammartino, president of Fairleigh Dickinson University, where I had taught a few courses in

58

English to the returned G.I.'s. "Don't worry about the future," he said. "We need you, we want you on the faculty. . . ." He had no job for me, I knew that: he hadn't the least idea of what he would do with me. He offered it not out of his good, executive mind, which knew better, but out of his heart, which knew only that I needed the therapy of a job offered even though I hadn't asked for it. All the words in the dictionary could not describe my gratitude for that letter; for the first time, I felt my feet really stepping out on solid rock.

Came the day when I went outside my room. It was as great an adventure as that of Christopher Columbus discovering America. I discovered the *rest* of the hospital. Don't forget, I had no conscious memory of ever having seen anything except my own room. Complete X-rays had to be taken and that meant a trip to the X-ray room. As soon as the arm came out of traction the great expedition took place. They put me on one of those little carts and the orderly went very slowly, so that I might see everything and everybody.

Have you ever looked out on the world from

a hospital cart? It is an amazing thing. People
and things you had forgotten existed spring into
life; the world widens and you see it as if from
a train window when the train turns a bend and
the horizon leaps back a hundred miles.

The room became a corridor—a long, shining, gleaming, new-looking corridor alive with
people who stopped to smile with joy as my
triumphal Caesar's chariot moved along. "Hi,
there! Look who's going for a ride!" It was short
—as short a distance as that from a prison cell
to the outer gate, but it was glorious. As I rode
around *my* hospital, being so proud of it, lines
from a poem I'd read long ago kept surging
through my mind:

I am a wanderer.
I remember well one journey,
How I thought the way was missed
So long the city I desired to see lay hid.
When suddenly its spires afar
Gleamed through the encircling clouds.
You can conceive my transport.
Soon the vapors closed again,
But I had seen the city,
And one such glimpse no darkness can obscure.

Author Unknown

THE BATTLE WITH FEAR

It wasn't such a glamorous city I had seen, but I had gone through tribulation to reach it, and I felt a kinship with sturdy adventurers everywhere.

A week later I sat in a chair. I was up. My right leg stood out in front of me stiff as a ramrod and I bit my lip at that, but I was up, and moving around—what did a stiff leg matter compared to that? At first the nurses wheeled me everywhere I wanted to go; then I began to drop my stiff right arm over the side of the chair and grasp the wheel, and push myself. It brought the thrill a child must get when he first stands on his own feet.

And then one day, after spring had come and gone and summer was half spent, they came and rolled me out of the building, outside, into the little hospital garden, out under the sky. That sky! It was filled with great billowing white clouds—a sky so deep and wide and blue, and high, high in it a small bird went winging. I sent my spirit winging after him. Free as a bird, free! I could not take my eyes from that sky and that bird; I could not gather into my heart all the beauty of it. I sang, to my own wild tune, the words of the 121st Psalm: "I will lift up mine eyes unto the hills, from whence cometh my help. . . ." The hills were roof tops, but what of that? It was my Father's singing, beautiful world, and I was in it and of it again.

In the churches of Granite City and Chatham the event was announced from the pulpits and thanksgiving prayers were offered.

But we human beings are very selfish beings. We are an unappreciative lot, individually and collectively. The fact that I was up and in a chair should have been enough to keep me lyrical with joy for days. It wasn't. A feverish dream, like a will-o'-the-wisp, lured me on into wishful thinking: When could I try to walk? Would it be with crutches? Or perhaps—daring thought—a cane? I spent dreamy hours planning the kind and design I would choose, if I would only be fortunate enough to use a cane and not a crutch. Week by week, the event was postponed. That fragmented pelvis had to be as strong as possible for the test. Finally, the day of days arrived and I was once more on my feet, perpendicular to the earth. To be sure, I was held there with the aid of a walker, but I was

upright. Not for long, of course. After a few minutes I was exhausted but deliriously happy.

The very next excursion in the walker an imp
must have gotten into my brain for when the
nurse left me alone for a moment, I left the
walker and launched out on my own, down the
corridor to the nurses' station. I thought I would
be greeted with cheers, but horrified stares gave
way quickly to a thoroughgoing tongue lashing.
Had I lost my mind? If I fell now, what a fall
that would be! I was whisked to bed in a hurry.

It was a foolhardy stunt to do, no doubt about
that, but it brought a sense of triumph and free-
dom that I needed, right then. I knew now that
I could walk; that my equilibrium was good. I
walked stiff-legged, yes—but I walked. I had
walked and not fainted.

"Crippled for life" had been a major fear in
all our minds from the first. At no time did Dr.
Bowers give us any encouragement which he did
not sincerely feel. We knew the problem of healing entailed a shattered pelvis which might—
very likely would—heal with a shortness in that
limb. We knew the knee might never stabilize
and might require steel braces so that I would

be able to stand upright. All these thoughts had been our constant, fearful companions.

Dr. Bowers came one day and measured carefully two or three times and announced the triumphant fact that my legs would be the same length. Such a victory of healing! And strength came into the knee in an amazing way. "You'll regain ninety per cent of its use," said doctor. It did not seem possible then, for the knee refused to bend. But if doctor said it could be done —it could! So now, one by one, we were saying good-bye to our "fearful companions."

There was still quite a battle to be fought with that leg, but the first skirmish with it had been won. And I had lost my fear of being permanently crippled—which is winning half the fight before the fight begins!

Chuck came, a little later, with his convertible. He picked me up in his arms, carried me out of the hospital and sat me down gently in the front seat. A *car*! I was frightened beyond belief. Not since the crash had I even dared think of an automobile. I could never do this, but I knew I had to. I couldn't spend the rest of my life being afraid of cars!

THE BATTLE WITH FEAR

A convertible was good, for in it I could look far and wide, as high as the sky and as wide as the horizon, and that means something to one who has been in a hospital for 110 days.

But there was still fear. My heart pounded as Chuck started the engine; I grasped the door so hard that my hands turned to chalk; perspiration stood out on my forehead and I closed my eyes as we began to move. In Granite City many of the streets come together in five corners, instead of four, and there was not a stop light in the whole town! Down those streets cars came rushing at us; I was sure every driver in every car *wanted* to hit us. The air rushed past my ears in a wild screech. Terror swept over and through me in nauseating waves, lasting for minutes. Then it would clear, and I'd open my eyes again.

Chuck drove slowly and watched me closely. He knew how hard it was; he also knew I had to do it. I was limp and exhausted when we got back to the hospital.

But we made it.

Now the end of the long hospital experience was approaching—now the time for me to leave was near. The last week was the happiest of them all. The ministers, who had done much for me, far beyond the call of duty, took me on short personally-conducted tours of the town; and I even went out, once, on a short shopping spree.

Sister Petronella asked me to go with her to a hospital Mass. As we knelt side by side in the little chapel I felt something damp touch my arm and hand, every now and then. In shy love, she was touching me with holy water; she wanted me to have that one last blessing as I went away.

No—there was one more blessing from Sister. She said to me, "I shall always keep you in my chalice." Her chalice—and her heart. It brought tears to my Protestant eyes.

Two ministerial students sent me an orchid the morning I left; I pinned it to my dress and thanked God for them and their thoughtfulness. I took one last, long look at my room—and I wanted to slam the door shut and lock it and *stay* there. It is childish, but we all feel that way; we love protecting walls, even when we suffer within them, and leaving a room in which we have lived means leaving a little of the heart.

But the laughter and joy of those around me

brought me out of this mood. I walked out gaily, as a conqueror should, shaking hands here, there, saying a good-bye that was joy mixed with tears. It was triumphant but teary glory.

The Horwiches took me to the station in St. Louis. The ride there wasn't so bad, but when I entered the enormous waiting room, fear took charge of me again and I trembled from head to foot. People rushed at me, past me, like a million wild horses in stampede. It was mad, chaotic, terrifying. I fought back an overwhelming desire to turn and run. I wanted to go back to the hospital, to the little room, to the gentle hands of those who had done everything for me for so long. This was the savage, murderous world that had tried to crush me; I was afraid of it and turned sick and faint. The noise, the dirt, the *confusion*. . . .

But then I remembered demerol, and I knew I could overcome this. A strong, sustaining power welled up from deep within me and I walked through the confusion and into the train. As it started and gained speed, I held on, every muscle tense. Then I looked out of the window.

Outside, in the late afternoon light, a golden

field of grain waved gently in the wind. Above it tossed a mass of cumulus clouds, billowing, snow-white, edged with pink and gold, against a laughing blue sky. Out of the depths of its beauty came a message from Pete, Jane and Jack like a telegram, with no conscious process of thought: "First step accomplished. Fear not for the next. Having a wonderful time. Wish you were here."

I was not there behind the sky with them; they were not here with me, alone in the roomette. Yet we rushed to each other over that invisible bridge of love, and we met and communicated with each other.

It was broken by the call of the porter: "Dinner now being served." I made my way to the diner, found a seat, and a waiter thrust a menu into my hands.

"Your order, ma'am?"

For 117 days, food had been thrust into my hands; I gave no orders about it. It was done for me, all of it. Now I had to decide about a meal.

I was back in the old world. I began to read the menu, and to drive my mind to decide what I would eat.

68

V

The Battle for High Ground

In the cool of the morning I stepped off the train in Wichita and into the arms of Dad Henry. His beautiful, strong face shone with joy and thanksgiving as his tears mingled with Mother Henry's and mine.

69

Coming to Wichita was like having God lay a cool hand on my forehead. It was an oasis; it was still waters and green pastures. It was a sweet interlude of peace and unspoken assurance, between the pain of yesterday and the uncertainty of tomorrow.

The house was quiet; the very air of this minister's home was filled with serenity and a faith that smiled. The world has great need of such hostels; they are the half-way houses between the horror of earth and the hallelujah of heaven.

But it was not altogether the fact that Dad was a minister that helped; nor so much what he *said* that made his thought or words impressive. It was that he had suffered, too. He had met the angel of death, before he ever knew me. Like Aaron and Hur, who held up the arms of Moses, he had known the battle: therefore he could help me through it. He spoke not out of books, professionally, but out of experience, humbly.

You who come walking feebly out of pain's prison—find someone like that for your convalescence. Find someone who has been through it, who knows because he has felt it.

Dad made no pretense of knowing all the answers, and for that I was thankful. Somehow, I am suspicious of people who try to explain life's problems of the deepest level in twenty minutes flat. I read once of a minister who said, "Every time I meet one of those fellows with glib answers to all the problems of life, I shake hands with him and congratulate him and get away from him as quickly as possible." I agree! There were some questions to which Dad Henry had no answer at all; there *were* no answers. I didn't want smooth explanations; I wanted understanding, and I got it.

It taught me a lesson. The best counselors in religion and pain, I think, are the best listeners; it is their listening, their willingness to sit in sympathy, and not their solutions, that kindles the warm glow around the heart.

Life became therapy, now—physical, mental, spiritual therapy. Every day we went to Wesley Hospital for a bout with my stiff right leg and knee. I joined a little company of strugglers who had been knocked off their feet and who were fighting fiercely just to stand up straight again. They were children and young adults who had had polio. I went there feeling sorry for myself, but all the self-pity in me melted at first sight of them. I became ashamed of myself, and proud of them. They had such courage and spunk and determination! They would try to walk and fail; they would slip and fall and get up and try again; they dragged their half-dead limbs around in heavy metal braces, fighting until the perspiration stood out on their foreheads and the tears ran from their eyes; and they wiped off the perspiration and the tears stood dry and salty on their cheeks and they tried again.

I commend it to you—you who have problems, you who think it "hard" to take a cut in salary or who feel alone and frustrated, and even you who have pain; I commend a trip to the nearest physical-therapy room. Go and take a good long look at the victims or look closely at their loved ones sitting around the walls of the room, their faces heavy with heart-pain, silent under the voices whispering that Jimmie or Jean may never make it, may never walk again. Try it sometime, you with "problems"—it will crush you, and lift you up.

The leg was a bitter obstacle; the fight with it in Wichita was in a measure worse than the fight with pain in Granite City. You can take drugs for pain, but you have to *make* a broken leg work. You struggle for hours, and the leg refuses to obey your commands; you lose your temper or, worse still, you lose your interest in making the effort, and the whole affair reaches an emotional impasse. You get so tired that your bones and muscles scream for rest. Then you try it just once more. Hours, days, weeks on end, you do that. Was it Franklin D. Roosevelt who said that when you had spent two years learning to wiggle your big toe, after polio, you could learn to do *anything*? I was learning. . . .

I spent the mornings at the hospital and the afternoons in bed, resting from the ordeal. There were mornings when I thought I could never get up. There were nights when I was too tired to sleep. This period is like that; you have your up days and your down days, your days of laughter and your days of teeth-clenching and lip-biting. What matters is that you keep going, that you stay in command of yourself and get out of that bed and get going again.

This you do for yourself and by yourself. God can't do all of it.

Do you remember Scarlett, in *Gone with the Wind*? Do you remember that, after the Civil War was over, she went back to Tara, her old plantation home, to find it ruined and the garden gone to seed and the whole place a burned desolation? Do you remember that she fell flat on her face in the garden and lay there clawing at the dirt in frustration and rebellion? She was the perfect picture of the broken South, as she lay there. . . .

But Scarlett got up. She got up and got out of there. She knew she *had* to get up, if she were to rebuild Tara and her life. There is no record in the book that she waited for God to come and pick her up, or that she asked Him to restore everything with one neat stroke of His hand. She got up under her own power and moved off under her own steam.

You've got to get up! You'll have help, once you try, but you must take that first step on your own. God and the world haven't much help to offer the coward who just wants to lie there and die.

So I got up; so I fought the leg until it loosed

and came free. What else could I do? What else could you do?

I began to take longer walks, and one fine morning I insisted upon going alone to the local supermarket, on an errand for Mother Henry. I was surprised to find out how difficult it was for me to go into that store. Buying food brought back memories. The small habits of my life as mother of a family came hurrying in upon me and I found myself automatically going over the food likes and dislikes of the children and the weekly buying program that had suited us best.

This is inevitable. In fighting to adjust ourselves to the loss of loved ones in death, we can prepare for the memories we foresee; it is the sight of the unexpected that hurts. The slip of paper falling out of a book, and the paper covered with familiar handwriting; the sight of a man who walks as your loved one walked; an unknown lad wearing a jacket like your lost lad's—do what you will, you cannot avoid these unexpected jolts. You just have to face them.

Getting up physically was difficult; getting up mentally and spiritually was even worse. That's where Dad Henry helped. He was a great listener—probably because he had been listening most of his life to tales of pain and woe. His approach was not "Now you listen to me, and I'll tell you what it's all about." It was a gentle "Come, let us reason together. . . ." Reason! It was the approach of common sense.

We went through a lot of books together, reading and analyzing and discussing; Dad matched his skilled theological mind against my more pedestrian one. We talked of the long pilgrimage of man and his search for a deepening, satisfying faith in the Judeo-Christian belief. I came to understand that Jesus, as the bridge between Hebraism and Christianity, had never once offered to *explain* the world; He had only offered triumph over it. I saw that the New Testament Christians got what He was driving at—that while they no more understood life than we understand it, they did find something in the spirit of Christ which enabled them to conquer its hardships. Others, I found, had walked the same bitter road that I was walking, and asked the same questions. They found good answers; I wondered if I could, too.

THE BATTLE FOR HIGH GROUND

And then I discovered Job. In the quiet of Dad's study I read again the story of his chastening—and of his friends, who offered so many suggestions to explain it. I got to chuckling as I read Job's answers to them. He would have none of their fancy philosophies; he was sharply sarcastic: "No doubt you are the people, and wisdom shall die with you!"

I read on in Job to find his sarcasm and despair turning to something better: "With him (God) is strength and wisdom." God, not man, has the answers; man only guesses at what God knows. I would have to look to God for the answers. I was content to go along with that.

I read, again, "In the thought of one who is at ease there is contempt for misfortune." It came over me that if I could or would give my mind completely to God, as Job did, then I could *despise* anything the world could do to me. When I reached that point, I had set my feet on the first high, solid ground since the days of the valleys of darkness. I had come to the place where I was beginning to trust God's mind to guide mine.

I read on in Job and came to the blast of

trumpets: "I know that my redeemer liveth," and "Though he slay me, yet will I trust in him!" (Trust in His wisdom, that is!) Job made sense. He made God a God of love, not a God of terror. I could accept that, especially inasmuch as it had come from one who had been deeper in the valley than I. Accepting it, the mists began to clear a little. I began to see that an attempt at cooperation with God would be a lot better than revolt against Him—a lot better than just blaming His "will" for everything, and ourselves for nothing.

It was good to renew acquaintance with Job, in Wichita.

These were days of rest, peace and returning strength. They were "just what the doctor ordered." What the doctor didn't order was the depressing thought, which forced itself into my mind day and night, that soon I would have to leave this haven and go back to the empty house in New Jersey.

An automatic half-thought would come, that I was just "visiting with the folks," and that my own family waited for me, back in Chatham. I was just "away" from them for awhile. Then the

78

hard fact would come roaring back at me that they were not in Chatham, and they would not be there when I went back, and that I *had* to go back. . . .

Wichita had been an oasis; now the time had come for me to face the desert again. I didn't know, as I boarded the plane for New Jersey, how much I would need Job and his trumpets.

VI

The Battle in the Mind

The storm would really break, I knew, when I tried to go back to the house which had been our home. It had assumed the proportions of Mount Everest in my mind; all the other fears I had known were minor foothills compared with this forbidding peak. I kept thinking of that title on one of Thomas Wolfe's books, *You Can't Go*

Home Again, and I realized I couldn't go *home* again. This was not home—this was only a house. The elements which had made it a home were gone and would not—could not—return. All that remained were the physical things a family had gathered unto itself in its process of making a home.

I remembered, too, that Dr. Bowers had said, "You won't break now. Not now. Not after what you've been through. You'll be all right." The confidence in his firm, resonant voice gave me the security I needed to try to climb "Everest."

Thanks to the wisdom and planning of Ed Parker, at whose home I stayed in Mountain Lakes before returning to Chatham, I approached it by degrees. One morning we went out for a drive; we just "happened" to drive through Chatham, where we called on Bill Rodda. The second time we drove around town a little; the third time we drove past the house. The fourth time, with Ed and his wife, Edith, and Bill Rodda, we went in.

Through one room, then another, and another. I entered no room alone; one of them was always with me when I stopped to look at a chair, or opened a door, or pulled out a drawer to look inside. I was never alone; they saw mercifully to that.

The house was fresh and bright; our friends had cleaned it from roof to basement. And from the calendars on the walls they had torn off the months of April, May, June, July and August—the lost, tragic months. Only the reminder of the present remained.

It was hard, but somehow not as hard as I had thought it was going to be. Pete, Jack and Janie were not there. As I look back at it now, I think God had a hand in the manner of my return. The folks in Kansas had planned to come back with me, but something happened to one after another of them, to prevent it. That was lucky for me—or providential—for if they had come, we should have lived together in the house, and that would have been agonizing.

As it was, the house turned out to be an empty shell; it was never a home again. I lived with friends in town while we sorted out and disposed of all that was within the walls of the house. As I rid myself of them, I kept saying, "You can't go home again—not back here! This *isn't* home; it is only a house that briefly sheltered a family. It's usefulness is over. Get rid of it."

Getting rid of "Everest" looked like a difficult job, a long session with real estate agents— but one day an elderly lady came ringing the doorbell. Was this house for sale? Well—I didn't just know—a nostalgic reluctance set in. I hesitated. She didn't.

"Beautiful! Just what I've been looking for!"

"But. . . ."

"I must have this house. When can I move in?"

She bought it, without the help of advertising, without benefit of real estate agents. Everest just collapsed, and disappeared from my life.

By mid-February I was enrolled at New York University, candidate for a Master's degree.

Working for this degree, I thought, would not only help me toward a good teaching position, somewhere; it would completely occupy my mind and force me outside of myself. I moved bag and baggage into New York City, and settled down to the long grind of the classroom.

I had never wanted to live in New York. It was too big, too impersonal, too commercial and greedy and dirty. Above all, dirty. The window of my little room looked out on the filthy roof of an *incinerator*! Beyond it stretched the roof tops of Greenwich Village—Sodom and Gomorrah rolled into one. I disliked it heartily, and to conquer my dislike and disgust I buried myself in an orgy of study. I plunged headlong into the world of the intellect, hoping that here I would find relief, and a norm to live by which, even if it couldn't answer the questions that still tortured my mind, might at least give me a philosophy with which I might struggle on.

My schedule included courses in all the usual subjects leading to an M.A. in English, with special emphasis on teaching those subjects in college. As I met my professors, one by one, I was overwhelmed by the understanding they gave me. I was only a name to them; they knew nothing of my background, but they knew something of my problems, and they were anxious to help. Rules were waived and I was allowed to take extra hours; they realized that I wanted to spend every waking hour in study. They went the limit in counseling with me, and in helping me to arrange my work; just to know these wise, mellow, brilliant professors as persons, in such a vast organization, was stimulating. One does not expect one of the largest universities in the world to be personal at any point, and when such human interest was found in my teachers, my heart was warmed.

The courses had exciting names: Humanitarian Literature, Literature and the Crisis in Human Values, and the inevitable, thought-provoking Educational Psychology.

I became a human blotter, absorbing the new knowledge made available in these courses. Or better still, I was a pool of water, and each drop of new knowledge set up wavelets of motion in my mind that started other waves of thought. New patterns developed; new conclusions were reached; inevitably, some of the old concepts died as the new ones were born. The surface of the pool seethed and bubbled with new ideas.

With some people, such a revolution might produce good results; with others, it can produce chaos and despair. It all depends on the person, and upon the moment when the tremendous change comes to him. There is a quality in events which, if they happen to individuals at one particular moment or period of their lives, will affect them as they would never be affected at other, more routine moments. It all depends on the circumstances.

For instance—if I had been taking these courses and going home every night to Pete and Jane and Jack, the "new knowledge" involved in them would have had little effect on me; I am sure of that. The environment of the home would have overwhelmed it all, and life would have gone on quite the same as it always had. But here I was alone—lonely, frustrated, unhappy, surrounded by strangers—and the impact was quite different.

Thus was set the stage for one of the major battles of my life.

A wise friend once said to me, "Bitterness is everywhere if you have it within yourself." I know that to be true. I found bitterness now because I was bitter inside. I embraced glittering new ideas, not because I had thought them through, but because my intellect had a warped perspective. I began to worship the new "rea-

son" in my kind, and the old faith began to wilt
and die. I accepted a reason unenlightened by
faith and God, and running wildly away from
Him.

It was no sudden descent; it was the result of
all the books I read and all the frank and free
classroom discussion of those books. Inch by
inch, those in the classroom slipped into the
seats of the cynics, the scornful. Out of the brilliant exchange of thought and concept came the
idea that man is an animal—no more, no less.
Sometimes he is a strong man, more often a
weakling; it was all a matter of how the genes
and the chromosomes happened to combine in
his physical make-up. It was all luck, all chance,
all accident. If you happen to have a healthy
body, you're lucky; it wasn't planned that way.
Nothing is planned. If you happen to be weak in
body and mind—well, you are weak, and there
is nothing you can do about it. You can just
expect to be run down, some day, in the rat-race
called life.

The reason I happened to be alive, I gathered,
was that I happened to be an unusually durable
piece of flesh; the genes and the chromosomes

had just, by pure accident, been good to me in making me a little stronger than run-of-the-mill humanity. I just didn't have sense enough to die. So, lacking in good sense, all I could do was to go on living and play my luck for all it was worth. Live it up! Eat, drink and be merry, for the time will come when my luck would run out, and I'd die, like all the rest of them, like a flea under a steam-roller.

Man is accident-prone, I learned. Crazy things happen to him, sooner or later. Out of the senseless world, some day, would come an accident that would cripple or kill. I couldn't prevent it. I might as well accept it, like a great, dumb elephant blundering into an elephant-gun in the jungle or a gay innocent pup running under a truck and getting himself crushed to death. It was all accidental. There wasn't any sense in any of it, and there surely wasn't any God. No power beyond the accidental and the human planned anything or helped anybody.

There was nothing spiritual in the accidental, animalistic world. Spirituality was for sissies, for the weaklings. Strong people with brains didn't need it. And we had brains.

88

THE BATTLE IN THE MIND

Brains crackled in all the classes. The students here were young, brash, sophisticated—*not* men mellowed by suffering, not sages with a wisdom forged out of life's disciplines. They were noisily sure that they were right in their materialistic intellectualism. They were healthy young animals. At first, I argued with them. I might as well have argued with the stone walls of the Empire State Building, uptown.

There were—to be fair—a few among them who felt somehow that man was something better than a mere animal in that he had a *power of choice*. They believed, not too deeply, that man was to a certain extent a moral as well as a physical creature, and not just so much dumb, sodden clay. But even these were pessimistic as to the end of man. They believed, with a cynical Melville, that "In tremendous extremities human souls are like drowning men; well enough they know they are in peril; well enough they know the causes of that peril; nevertheless, the sea is the sea, and these drowning men do drown!" We all drown, eventually. There is no escape from it. We just drown.

But I had always believed with a Melville of

more optimistic mood that "There is an ever up-bubbling of wickedness—but also, *one can see the ever-beckoning star*." This had meant, to me, a going out and going on in faith. To my new friends in the classroom, that was nonsense. Faith was for fools. Intellectually, they were more astute than I was in the things of the visible world; I realize now that they were immature and completely lost when they came to the level of the unseen. They just drowned there!

It was an acid bath into which I had plunged, and the acid burned. Every morning I would wake up hoping that this day the sun would break through, and every night I went to bed convinced there was no sun at all. It got me down and kept me down. I was caught in a whirlpool of cynicism, spinning until I was dizzy, going lower, lower all the time, going deeper, going under. . . . The vortex of the whirlpool was controlling me, and the "rational" was in the ascendancy. The faith in me was being slowly drowned.

To make it worse, there were the anniversaries. In February came the anniversary of Jane's birthday; that day and night I thought would

90

never end. In March, a year ago, she had left us, and in April came the anniversary of the crash which took "accident-prone" Pete and Jack. Such memory-laden days were constant. I wandered the streets, forlorn, lost, ready to scream my bitterness. I looked at women with husbands and laughing children, and I hated them. It was the bottom of the pit. Why, I reasoned, should I go on fighting? Why bother to live?

I contemplated suicide and its attractive simplicity. The ending of one's life is so easy; it is the going on living that is difficult. Time and again I stood frozen on subway platforms and watched the trains come roaring into the stations; time and again I longed to throw myself under the wheels and end the fight; time and again I put the firm substance of a subway pillar between myself and the train, and cringed behind it. You call it weakness. Perhaps it was. But anniversaries can be unbelievably brutal, when you have to face them alone. Your friends are not always there to help. . . .

It seemed to me that nobody cared. I was certain I didn't care. I lived only because I didn't have sense enough to die. Some day, somewhere, somehow, I would die. Why not now? Why wait?

This was where the "reasonable" approach had brought me. I was living a bitter, solo existence. I was frightened, insecure, and above all, alone. All around me was the "ever up-bubbling of wickedness," in sprawling, tawdry New York. It is hard to see the "ever-beckoning star" from under the bright lights of Broadway.

One day as I crossed Washington Square I saw a gang of shouting lads take a cat and smash it against a tree. As they went into gales of laughter over that, I was so sick I couldn't move. I cried out in my heart, "God—*why?* Why did you take gentle Jack, and let these monsters live?" In that moment I almost went down for good. I almost accepted the philosophy of the intellectuals in my classroom. What was the use of going on?

Then, in the very darkest hour, there came to me thoughts out of a book I had read five long years before. They were the words of Alec R. Vider, in a book called *Christian Belief*: "The trial of man is proceeding now and all the time.

The ground of the Bible's belief in immortality is not that the human soul must go on, but that life in God and especially in the risen Christ cannot cease. We who are Christians work out a system of faith which is a personal trust in Christ. There remains a very dark world of which Christ is the light, and a Christian need not pretend it is otherwise."

Why did I recall such words *at such a time*? Why, out of all I had read and studied, did this thunderbolt statement of immortality and trust in Christ come back to me? You explain it, if if you can. I do not try to explain it; I accept it as an evidence of the outreaching of the communion of the saints, of the presence of an invisible influence and spirit in human affairs.

We were moving into the holy season of Lent and Easter, and the voices of Lent and Easter came through. I still do not know *how*; it still seems that the walls of the new ideas I had accumulated were too high and solid for those old holy voices to conquer, but conquer they did. The voices of Easter were simply stronger in me than the voices of the new reason, and they won.

Perhaps it was because the seeds which had

93

been planted in my childhood by my minister father now burst into bloom in my maturity; perhaps it was that in the depths of my heart and mind the cold intellectualism of the classroom had never quite overwhelmed the conviction that there was a heart and mind of creative love in the universe. Whichever it was, it drove me to every church service I could find time to attend. I heard Bach's tenderly dramatic *St. Matthew's Passion*, and Mendelssohn's tremendous *Elijah*. I let the soul-stirring words flow through me: "Oh, rest in the Lord; wait patiently for Him. And He shall give you your heart's desires. Oh, rest in the Lord."

I sat in a pew and told myself, "Iona Henry, when you could do nothing, the Lord took excellent care of you. You did not call the ambulance that took you to a good hospital, skilled in handling accident cases. You did not send for Dr. Bowers, whom the Lord equipped with special skill. You did not. . . ."

The list stretched on and on. . . .

God's care of me *had* been thorough and complete; why should He forsake me now? He would not; of that my soul was certain. I was the one who was doing the forsaking—not He! My heart's desires—would He give me those? Now I had the patience to wait, and see.

I left that singing of *Elijah* with God's manna falling on my spirit and the words, "I can do all things through Christ who strengthens me," a litany in my soul. As in the days in the hospital, Christ was again the catalyst through whom strength and power flowed from God to me.

That night I went out to Chatham, to a Communion service. It was an old tradition in the town, with all the Protestant churches participating. That participation, that sharing of the Lord's Supper, had always appealed to me as a splendid community effort. But tonight it was personal. The majestic beauty of the ancient ritual seemed created just for *me*. I seemed to be hearing my beloved father repeating the words, "It is very meet, right, and our bounden duty that we should at all times and in all places give thanks unto thee, O Lord, Holy Father, Almighty, Everlasting God." And another memory overwhelmed me: I felt at my side the presence of Pete, Jane and Jack, repeating with me the response: "Therefore with angels and archangels, and with all the company of heaven, we laud and magnify thy glorious name . . . heaven and earth are full of thy glory." Full of God's glory! The communion of the saints! It was here, at this Holy Communion. The family was with me. How could I forsake *them*? How could I disappoint them in an act of selfish suicide?

I got up out of my pew, walked down the aisle and knelt at the altar rail. *It was the first time since the day of the accident that I had been able to bend my right knee in a full kneeling.*

It was not so much a kneeling as a leap—a leap from the midnights of doubt to the triumphant victory of Easter. As I sang the old hymns in the beloved church on Easter Sunday, I knew the strife was not entirely "o'er," that the battle was not yet done. It would go on, I know not how long. But now I could sing with conviction, "The victory of life is won; the song of triumph has begun. Allelujah!" It was a new birth of faith. It had come through a perilous passage, but it and I were safe now, and it was good to find myself in the hands of God. Never again would suicide seem a logical answer; no more would reason sit enthroned alone. I demanded of myself that reason and faith rule together—and thus ended the battle with the mind.

Yet, glorious as it was, I knew that not all the demons had been exorcised. There would be hours of bitterness, in the future, and loneliness, and the desire for a reasonable meaning of my work and labor. These were still lurking on the perimeter of my being and might overwhelm me at any moment. But I was alone no longer. I had started up the shining path of faith.

Satisfied now that God was with me, I had one more step to take; to put myself in complete communion and cooperation with Him.

VII

The Last High Hill

September found me on the campus of Pfeiffer College, properly equipped with my Master's degree and ready to teach.

Other schools had beckoned, nearer home and friends, but Pfeiffer seemed best. It was small, which would be a relief from overcrowded

N.Y.U.; it was in an unfamiliar part of the country, which would be stimulating. And it was church-related, which meant that it would be faith-centered—and I needed that.

It was good, that college. To me it was the kindliest campus in America. The faculty and administration were friendly and the students were something you meet once in a lifetime: lively, wholesome, eager, happy and with an innate goodness of spirit that took hold of me and lifted me up. They were Jack and Jane to me. . . .

On the gloomiest days they would call from outside my little apartment, "Hey, Mrs. Henry. How's the coffee?" It was like having God Himself put out a friendly hand. The students, the lovely Carolina hills, the mockingbird in the tree beyond my window, the color and movement and hope and faith and eagerness of life —these were the ingredients of God's tonic for my sick heart.

There was a lingering sickness, though. It was that heart-sickness which hangs on like the aftermath of some stubborn disease.

Two words seemed indelibly written in my

mind; they were "Yes . . . but!" I was launched on a new profession—teaching. Yes —but I hadn't chosen it; it was forced upon me. I was enjoying the beauty of a new American landscape, yes—but I could have seen that anyway. I was absorbing a new culture, yes—but I could have done that as wife and mother. I was helping others, yes—but I could have done that in Chatham!

Yes, *but!* It was selfish, and it was depressing.

And the old question, "Why?" was not entirely gone, as I had thought at Easter. Added to it was another: "What?" What am I doing here? Away from all my friends and folks, for a whole year? What sense did all this exile make? I'd sit in faculty meetings, toward the close of day, and unbidden the thought would come, "What am I doing here? I should be home, getting dinner for the family."

A woman alone in the world is terribly alone. However kind her friends, she can still be an isolated human island, putting one foot before the other, day after day after day. It is the monotony, the grueling loneliness that crushes her spirit. Shakespeare must have been thinking of this tedious rhythm when he wrote:

> *Tomorrow, and tomorrow, and tomorrow,*
> *Creeps in this petty pace from day to day*
> *To the last syllable of recorded time,*
> *And all our yesterdays have lighted fools*
> *The way to dusty death.*

In spite of the victory of the last Easter, there were still days like that. There are such days for all who know sorrow and the readjustment it inevitably brings. There are mountain-peak days and deep-valley days, and fiery-furnace times, and the soul can face them as a soldier in the heat of battle. But then come the long, utterly endless days which stretch on and on in the same monotonous agony; they are the days of testing for the soul. *If* you can learn patience and hold fast to hope through such days—*you'll make it!*

I was learning—the hard way.

But, as usual, help came. It was in the beloved attitude of the students, and the sound of sympathy and cheer in their voices. Often, in my hours alone, I had the inspiration of great music; the Requiems of Mozart and Brahms and Verdi were particularly helpful. Their words consoled me: "As one whom his mother comforteth, so will I comfort you. . . ." "Blessed are they that mourn: for they shall be comforted." "Blessed are the dead which die in the Lord. . . ." "They that mourn and the blessed dead are separated only by the twinkling of an eye and are at rest with the Lord."

The words healed, for they told me that the family circle was still complete and unbroken, in spite of death. My lost ones were not lost; they were at Pfeiffer with me.

I taught a Sunday school class, and that helped. And I sat one day in college chapel and at long last saw the shining path open before my eyes. A singing gladness came over me and set me free. It was the quick, unexpected shout of victory at battle's end—it was reaching the top of the last high hill.

I stood there and looked back at the road I had traveled, at the little minor hills and valleys, at battles won and battles lost, at the countless little defeats that had to come before the sudden victory was mine.

Suppose we look back at it together. . . .

102

(I pray now that I may not offend, for I know that not all who read this will agree. I know that some have found comfort where I did not, and I rejoice for them that they have found their way out. This is my experience, the way that worked for me.)

I had tried many doors of escape, looked down many roads that seemed to offer the illusive shining way; they all turned out to be dead end. There was, first of all, the way of the planned pattern: "There is a purpose in all of this." The idea was that I had been saved out of the holocaust for some hidden, unknown, unknowable purpose. What that purpose was I could never know, and was not expected to know. God had put a blindfold on my eyes. It was a traditional Protestant idea; it has its roots in the doctrines of predestination. It was, I think, of certain value to me in my moments of deepest pain; the psychology of it was good *then*. But as I tried to follow it during convalescence, I found that it brought me up against a brick wall. Purpose? What purpose could there possibly have been in taking Pete and Jack and Jane, who had so much more to contribute than I? If

103

there was a purpose, why couldn't God, why shouldn't God reveal it to me? Why hide it? It left me desolate and unhappy. It explained nothing.

A friend at the hospital had gone further with this idea: she had told me that "God loves you, so He makes you suffer." God cared a great deal for me, so He gave me a great deal to bear. My friend was speaking, of course, out of the doctrine her church had taught her: those who suffer greatly earn great "merit," which speaks for them in the life to come, and provides a passport to happiness there. The more suffering here below, the more joy over there. Be glad you suffer now, for you will be so much happier later.

But, my mind reasoned, few ever suffered as I had suffered. Some perfectly good people never seemed to suffer at all. Why pick on me? Why didn't *everyone* go through the same school of pain? Why me? Was I selected, out of all humanity, for this? *Did God love me so much more than He loved the others?* I couldn't believe that. My faith had taught me that God has no caste system, that He plays no favorites and has no pets, that He sends His blessed rain upon just and unjust alike, that His love and mercy are given to all and not to a privileged few. I just couldn't accept the philosophy of "God punishes you because He loves you!"

It was similar, in some ways, to another philosophy offered by other friends: that I was a sort of substitute for them, as Christ had been substitute for all of us. I wondered why I had been picked as the substitute. And where was *my* substitute? What would happen to these good friends of mine, to their explanation, if and when sorrow came to them—as it might very well come? It was another explanation that didn't explain; it melted quickly, like snow in the sun.

There were those who came to me with the shining face of Pollyanna. They patted my shoulder and said, "Never mind. It's all right. Everything will be all right. Just don't worry about it." That infuriated me. It wasn't all right, and they knew it, and I knew it. This came usually from those who had known little if any suffering. It was too glib, too pat. Pollyanna and I had never been very good friends and we couldn't seem to manage any better now than before.

105

Others said it was just "fate." They believed in the hidden purpose and they went a step further: they paid tribute money to the goddess of Chance. "When your time comes," they said, "you just have to accept it." It reminded me of the fatalism of the soldiers who say, "When the shell comes over with your name on it—well, it's just yours, that's all." This extremity was sickening. There was nothing new about it; the Apostle Paul may have had it in mind when he warned us to beware of soothsayers and fortune-tellers. The "fate" pattern was easy to reject. I couldn't believe that God played ducks and drakes with us for awhile, amusing Himself with our struggles until He wearied of it, and then with one wild stroke of His hand smashed the life out of us. What possible pleasure could He get out of that? The God I knew and loved was not a God of the smashing hand, but One with a lifting hand.

One of the most persistent philosophies which had been advanced was that of the theory of good and evil: there is in this world a power for good (God) and a power for evil (the devil). I had been unfortunate enough to come under the

106

power of the evil one, who had "let me have it."
It was like the devil afflicting Job with his boils
(and keep it clear that it was the devil and not
God who did this). Allied with this idea was the
idea of "balances"—that life in general is balanced between good and evil, joy and pain,
health and sickness. You get so much good out
of it, and so much unhappiness, and eventually
they even up. Of course, this is more pagan than
Christian. The old pagan worshipers were forever placating the gods and goddesses of this
and that, in an effort to fend off their wrath.
Mothers threw their babies into the fiery furnaces of Moloch; the Aztecs offered human sacrifices to appease a terrible god. It seemed to me
that if we were to accept this philosophy, and go
the limit with it, we would be more primitive and
uncivilized than intelligent and Christian.

Yet the problem of the presence and power of
evil in our world is real, and not to be laughed
off lightly by simply calling it pagan. It is found
in countless references in the Bible, and it is found
in the words of Jesus. It is a problem that has
had the attention of twenty centuries of Christian scholars. The problem is still unanswered;

perhaps it is unanswerable. I certainly have not settled it, nor do I hope to. But I do know this: if too much emphasis is put upon the presence of evil in the world, and if this is your only answer to the question, "Why did this happen to *me*?" you will develop a pessimistic, almost hopeless attitude toward life. It leaves too much to chance, and it leads straight to fatalism.

The philosophy of materialism I have already described. It was fatalism, and worse, in New York, for it recognized no God worth recognizing. It was a complete denial of everything Christian; it exiled God from His world and left His children not something a little lower than the angels but something hardly higher than the beast. Whatever God there may have been in this philosophy was a weakling. Chaos was master in the world, and "the reins of the universe are tangled in the frantic hands of God." It was the picture of God trying to control things that were out of control; He may have had some secret purpose in mind, but He was helpless to halt the slaughter inherent in the chaos. That I could never accept, for, to me, if God is intelligent enough to create a universe, He is certainly intelligent enough to guide and control it. Down that

108

road, at least for me, lay nothing but nihilistic despair.

There had been some who felt that I should get the help of a good psychiatrist. Possibly one might have helped; they help a great many people. But my problem seemed to call for the aid of someone who had battled through difficulties like mine, as Christ had battled through to the cross. I think God sent me to Wichita and the quiet hours in Dad Henry's study, where I came to a very deep appreciation of Christ on that cross.

Dad Henry's philosophy was the first that really stood the test. He taught me to look at the whole thing in the light of plain, ordinary common sense, in the light of an orderly universe that ran under the reins of law. When we break that law, either consciously or unconsciously, we pay the penalty for breaking it. When we live in cooperation with the law, even though we do not always understand it, we live well and securely. It was the philosophy of a mature mind, of human understanding coupled with the divine compassion of the Lawmaker. This I could not grasp, at first.

If God were running things, I asked bitterly,

why hadn't He kept us in that restaurant a few minutes longer, the morning of the crash? If we'd stayed there just two more minutes, the whole thing would never have happened. *Why?* Dad's reply was something like this:

"Some things happen in this world because we human beings act like human beings, not because God makes them happen. Just because your car got to that railroad crossing at the very moment the train reached it doesn't mean that God planned it that way. God makes certain laws. He gives men the know-how to create automobiles and locomotives and to drive them at certain speeds. But it is *human* planning and decision that bring a car and a locomotive to a certain spot at a certain time. That's the working of the human will, and you can't expect God to reach down out of high heaven to stop the car or the train, once their human drivers have set them in motion. That would be to deny all the laws of movement and locomotion—*and it would deny the right of the human being and the human will to make decisions, as well.*

"It's like a soldier being killed in battle. If man creates the battle and the war, and places

110

himself deliberately out where the bullets are flying, then he creates the possibility of being struck by one of the bullets. He has no right to expect God to stop the bullet, once man has pulled the trigger! What a confused madhouse life would be, if God were to interfere like that!

"No, it wasn't God's will or decision that the crash should happen. *It is not God's will that you suffer!*"

It fell into my heart like rain on parched ground. How long I had waited to hear that! I had longed to believe it, but I had not thought through to it, as he had. Not one in a million of us think it through; it's so much easier to say, "Oh, it's just God's will." We seem to know more about His will than He does, at times! I think it's a quite inadequate answer.

I had been struggling toward this idea that God doesn't follow us around with a whip in His hand ever since I had first become acquainted with the philosophy of "God tests your faith by punishing you."

This philosophy made me furious. It seemed as ghastly, in my case, as the slaughter of the little children who laughed at Elisha's bald head.

If God "chasteneth" as a father spanking a child for the child's own good—all right! I could understand that. But to think that God would brutally *murder* Jane and Pete and Jack just to punish me was just too horrible for me to believe. The God I love, loves; He is no murderer, no sadist taking delight in inflicting pain.

Dad's philosophy, I think, is best expressed in a letter he wrote us while we were waiting to find out whether Jane's tumor was benign, or fatal. He wrote that he was praying that it would not be malignant and fatal, but that if it were. . . .

Perhaps this will help you now:

First: Whatever happens, life must go on for you. There are too many friends and loved ones depending on you to do otherwise. Whatever happens to us, the stream of life must flow on. So take good care of yourselves and don't give way to total defeat. Much in life is for you and with you whatever comes. Keep this firmly fixed, these days.

Second: Don't give way to "what might have been." We are apt to do so. We are apt to think that

112

if we had known sooner or if we had done differently, it would not be this way. But this is a region without boundary lines. It might not have changed results one bit. Don't linger there. You have done and are doing all you can in every way you know. Leave it there, for this is all any of us can do in life.

Third: God is as sad over this as you are. It is not God's will that such things happen. Amid the many circumstances of life, some things happen because we belong to a human society. But God's will is for life to be lived to its fullness. When it isn't, He stands as of old, weeping with us.

Fourth: We Christians believe in immortality. Whatever is commenced here will be completed there. *Nothing is lost* out of His care.

It clicked! This was a realistic, sensible philosophy. It had held like a rock in the melancholy maelstrom through which I had struggled in New York, and it was part of the foundation of the more reassuring faith I had found at Easter.

All this I had been through; all these philosophies I had pondered, accepted or rejected by the time I came to the Pfeiffer campus. I was still turning it all over in my mind as I sat one morning in college chapel. Suddenly it came; suddenly, the mists rolled back and the shining path

113

broke open before my eyes. I saw it clearly. Perhaps it was the long desperate working-out or working-together of all the philosophies suddenly melting into one, as the result of mental struggle, mental acceptance and rejection. Or perhaps it was a sudden insight that had nothing whatever to do with all that. Whatever it was, it came like a bolt of lightning.

The answer was *this*:

"Whatever is, is: you cannot change it. Whatever *has* happened, has happened, and you cannot go back and change any of it, however or 'whyever' it happened. The question is not 'Why did it happen?' but 'What do I do *now*?' Sit and fight it, all the rest of my life? Sit and rebel and weep and gnash my teeth? That will not help at all. The thing to do, wherever I am, is to do the very best I can and to leave the rest to God. If I had been put here to be a mother, then I should be the very best mother I could be; if I had been put here to run a business, then I should run that business well. If I had been put here to be a teacher, then let me be the best possible teacher!

"Stop fighting, Iona Henry! Stop questioning everything. Some questions have no answer; you should know that by now. You should know that only fools persist in seeking the answers to 'Why?' You will batter yourself to death asking for the impossible. Put your hand in the hand of the God you *know* is there.

"Stop asking, 'What am I doing in North Carolina?' Stop insisting that you will do what you want to do, like a spoiled, sulking child, and do what you *must* do. What must be done may seem impossible, but God has a way of working out the impossible. Do your part; do what must be done *and do it well.*"

It was so clear! It was not a case of what I wanted to do but of what, with God's help, I had to do. I had wanted to shut myself up in the little house that my selfishness had built, and die. "Move out of it," said God. "Go to work and improve your skills. You *can* sing the Lord's song in a strange land, if you want to."

The words of William Alexander Percy rushed into my mind:

Oh, I have heard a golden trumpet blowing
Under the night. Another warmth than blood
Has coursed, though briefly, through my intri-
cate veins.

115

TRIUMPH OVER TRAGEDY

Some sky is in my breast where swings a hawk
Intemperate for immortalities
And unpersuaded by the show of death.
I am content with what I cannot prove.

A strange complete new peace and relaxation flooded over me such as I had not known since the fearful trial began. It was like finding a bridge over a river in flood. Once, in Scotland, I had watched the fog lift from the bridge over the Firth of Forth. The span had been buried in the mists of early morning, and I could see only the towers high above the water. But when the fog lifted I could see the great stone piers of the bridge firmly rooted in the land on either shore and the strong, steel rails leading across. This experience in the Pfeiffer chapel was somehow like that. I saw now not only the two earthly piers that were common to all men—the twin experiences of birth and death—but the long bridge of faith which God had built between

116

them. The bridge had always been there; I had not seen it, for the fog. Isaiah spoke to me in the chapel: "I girded thee, though thou hast not known me." The bridge, the undergirding arms of God, had been there all the time!

The little questions turned and ran; they were not important any more. The tension went out of me; the strain eased. I was completely relaxed.

Call it what you like; I call it the philosophy of relaxed *rapport*. Or relaxed *harmony* with God.

It is not a "do nothing but believe" philosophy; it calls for action. It is not retreat or just giving up something you cannot understand; it is a challenge to go on. It is a mature attitude toward God, an alliance with a power greater than you are or ever can be, but a power that, nevertheless, respects you. It is an attitude of mutual respect and love. Of course God loves you; else why would He have bothered to create you?

It does not mean hopeless resignation. It does not mean going out to the cemetery every day to weep over something you cannot change; it does not mean shutting yourself up to weep and curse

117

God and die. It *does* mean enlarging your talents and gifts and going to work with them.

It does mean coming to terms with what God wants you to do, and doing it. It means knowing that so long as you do your part, God will do His. It is accepting the fact that what often seems to be wrong often turns out to be right—in God's wisdom, if not in yours.

I call it relaxed rapport; actually, it is going-onness.

I thought of Pete and Jane and Jack going on —not as the victims of inexplicable tragedy, but crossing bridges of their own, developing, growing. They were on an adventure that was far greater than mine; it did not have the physical limits of mine!

And I am going on, as well as they. I had not been halted in my development; I had not been condemned to spend the rest of my life in shallows and in miseries; as my body had been healed, so my spirit. I was led out upon a new road of life, hand in hand with Christ.

I had come at last to that: to a new walk with Christ. All else had failed. All my little philosophies had crumbled one by one under the bitter rain of reality, but this one stood the test. It was founded upon rock, and Christ was the rock.

It seemed to me like the candles of Tenebrae —that amazing worship service of the church in which thirteen lighted candles symbolizing Christ and His apostles are snuffed out one by one, until the only light left in the great, darkened church is that one little flickering candle of Christ. It had happened to me. One by one the little flickering schemes I worked out had failed me and plunged me back into the dark, completely baffled by the mystery and the inexplicable nature of things, until there was only one left, this one light left burning.

The great glory of it was that this light could not go out. It had flickered desperately in more dark ages than one, but always, after men and their storms had done their worst, it still burned. It flares into high flame every Easter; it burns steadily through all the year, if we have but eyes to see it. Christ Himself has promised that it will not go out, whatever happens. I rest content, relaxed, in that.

I know now that God has never promised me —nor any of us—exemption from suffering. But

He does promise the companionship of the light! And He has provided compensations in my life, which I discover daily, in my going on. The spirit which could see no light now sees the shining path.

So I believe in God. I believe in God Almighty, who out of His almightiness created me and gave me power to help Him become yet more almighty.

I believe in His Son, Jesus Christ; He is my Helper, Mediator, Saviour, Guide; He is the divine catalyst in my soul and life. As I believe in His going-onness after His crucifixion and death, I believe that we all go on. I believe that the dead, with Him, are alive, going on.

I believe in the Holy Spirit in life. I think of this Spirit as God in action in my life. I believe it is, or can be, the great driving power of life; I believe that it came to me through the words and works of Christ, and that it has power enough to make everything new. I believe this not because of any intellectual conviction, but because I have found it at work in my own living. I have not called down the Holy Spirit; the Spirit has come to me of its own will and desire.

120

I believe in the Communion of the Saints. I believe that those who have "gone on" communicate with us out of their wider area of understanding, and that neither they nor we are limited by bodily characteristics, nor by time, nor space.

I believe in immortality, in the going-on of the human personality. I believe that there is an indefinable, intangible spiritual content in all of us which can never die. I believe this is the real "you," and that this "you" is eternal; it learns a bit in this phase called life and goes on to learn more in the next phase of life. (I distrust those terms, "this life" and "the next life"; it is all one life, one eternity. We are living in eternity *now*; we are students in a school which knows no last session.)

This to me is not reincarnation; that means confinement to this earth, not an on-goingness that is universal. We are to go on with a changed, improved, spiritual body. So I pray for my loved ones as I pray for those about me on this earth, and my prayers are an expression of my love for them and my care for their adventure—that they may make the most of it. I pray for their

121

help, too, in my adventure here—that I may not take it like a frightened, blundering baby. It is a two-way proposition, just as it was when they were with me in the flesh.

I believe that, being physically constituted as we are, pain is inevitable for all of us. We are flesh, soft flesh, and we cannot possibly escape being cut on one or another of the barbs of life. I also believe that we can learn much in being cut, and that for every pain there is healing and compensation. This is not a surrender to the "good and evil" theory; it is a facing-up to a reality that sometimes hurts.

I believe that the Creator gave us minds with which to think, to search and find, to ask questions. What could be more stupid than a child with no questions about life, than a grown man or woman who is completely unconcerned with all that happens around him or her? God gave us brains to use, and not as terminals for our spinal cords. And I think He wisely put some things forever just beyond the grasp of the finite mind, so that we might never become self-satisfied "know-it-alls" but always seeking, seeking, seeking. Who has any respect for a religion without mystery, without unexplored country to explore?

This I believe because it has come to me tempered and strong out of the fiery furnace of my trial. This I believe because it has become a faith that works, that has taken from me all tension and bitterness and given me a sense of relaxed harmony with God. It has also put into my hands some of the fruits of the spirit—a bountiful harvest which grows richer every day. I do not have all the fruits secure in my "basket," and how prone I often am to spill the contents and go wandering in the dark valleys *without* love and peace and patience and all the rest of it! The process is not complete, but it is going on. Some days bring shattering battles; some days are unbearably long; unbidden, searing memories do return.

But those memories no longer have the power over me that they once had. I have a weapon to fight them with, now.

This I believe because it makes sense where other philosophies made nonsense. It makes sense because only faith in a caring, loving, impartial God makes sense. It is not reasonable for me to think that God gives life and light to creative human minds—to a Raphael, a Brahms, a Newton—only to drop them in a grave at the end of threescore years, more or less, with a "That's all. This is the end." Why should He bother to create us at all, if *that* is the end? A creative energy which could be *that* wasteful is not much of a force to worship, or be guided by, or even to love. Will I shock you when I say that I—or you—could have devised a better system than that, and organized a more competent use of human material?

But the solid fact is that I could not have devised man and the universe as they are, nor could you.

A mind beyond, greater than anything we tiny Lilliputians could conceive of, brought all that into being, in a most orderly way.

It is for us to fit into the order, not for the order to fit *us*.

So at long last the question of "Why?" gave over to another: "Where? Where now? Where shall I go to do the work I must do?" No longer do I need to know why.

Perhaps, as the years roll on, one or another

of the *details* of this relaxed rapport philosophy will change, for I know that truth grows. But only the outer edges of it, I think, will change; the hard core of it will remain. Whatever old concept I drop or whatever new idea I adopt, this will remain as it is, as it has always been.

Nothing can hurt me, any more.

I know, and deeply, what M. Louise Haskins means when she writes:

> *And I said to the man who stood at the gate of the year:*
> *"Give me a light, that I may tread safely into the unknown!"*
> *And he replied:*
> *"Go out into the darkness and put your hand into the Hand of God.*
> *That shall be to you better than light and safer than a known way."*
> *The Gate of the Year.*

For I have walked far in the valleys of the unknown land, and I have come safely through.